Disney

D1491382

Alexander Kennedy

Amazon.com/author/alexanderkennedy

Contents

Prologue

Around Hollywood, they called the project "Disney's folly." The newspapers might be willing to believe Walt Disney could do anything, but those within the industry were skeptical. Even Disney's wife and brother, Lilian and Roy, tried to talk him out of the project. But Walt was unshakeable; his studio would produce the world's first full-length, cel-animated film, or go down trying.

There was no pressing need for the experiment—only his own ambition. His creation of Mickey Mouse, for whom Disney himself did the early voice work, had been a major success, replacing Oswald the Lucky Rabbit, which a former business partner had wrested away (a betrayal that Disney never forgot, nor forgave). Disney Studios now turned out shorts for its *Silly Symphonies* series like clockwork, many of them of extraordinarily high quality. In 1932, Disney had been the first to bring cutting-edge, three-strip Technicolor to the big screen, even signing a deal for three years of exclusive rights to the process. In 1933, his studio produced *The Three Little Pigs*, with its iconic song, "Who's Afraid of the Big Bad Wolf?" It was a runaway success, eventually becoming the most successful animated short film of all time.

But like any true innovator, Disney was never satisfied to repeat his past successes. Now that his studio had mastered the animated short, he wanted to break new ground with an animated feature. Later, after his studio had become the undisputed king of the animated feature, Disney found himself restlessly turning to television, creating the runaway hits *Davy Crockett* and *The Mickey Mouse Club*. Having become a ratings champion in television, he turned his attention to real-life attractions, creating the world's most visited amusement parks. And so it went until his death.

In 1934, however, these challenges and accomplishments still lay in the future. When Disney announced to the newspapers that his studio would be the first to put an animated feature film on the screen, it's understandable that many competitors thought they had heard the last of Disney Studios.

Disney knew that the challenges involved would be immense, though the reality proved even worse than he had imagined. All told, the final film required more than 160,000 individual paintings, and the animators produced more than 2 million images in the course of the project. Disney initially estimated the cost to the studio would be around $150,000 to $250,000, but before it was done, the film actually cost almost $1.5 million.

Yet Disney understood that the worst thing he could do was rush his project or try to do it cheaply. He began with the remarkable step of sending his animators (many of whom were newly hired for this project) to art classes to practice drawing human anatomy. One of Disney's regular animators spoke years later of the importance of the professional training they received from one of their instructors, Don Graham:

He taught us things that were very important for animation. How to simplify our drawings—how to cut out all the unnecessary hen scratching amateurs have a habit of using. He showed us how to make a drawing look solid. He taught us about tension points—like a bent knee, and how the pant leg comes down from that knee and how important the wrinkles from it are to describe form. I learned a hell of a lot from him!

Meanwhile, Disney and his writers began plotting the movie. He wanted to animate the fairy tale of Snow White, he told them. The story had been previously considered for a subject of one of their famous *Silly Symphonies*, but Disney had decided to hold back the idea for a longer feature. In particular, he thought the seven dwarves had enormous comic potential, and they were soon added to the film's title: *Snow White and the Seven Dwarves*.

Compared to the intricate plotting of a modern-day Disney Studios movie like *Frozen*, Disney's early approach to features was more improvisational. He tended, understandably, to view the features as composed of strung-together shorts. The plots of *Snow White* (1937) or *Bambi* (1942) could be written out on a napkin without leaving much out, and *Fantasia* (1940) was a literal anthology. Instead of working from a top-down outline, then, Disney let the story grow in a bottom-up fashion, allowing the film to grow out of various gags, bits, and scenes; at one point, he offered his writers $5 for each "gag" they generated. Both writers and animators were required to watch scenes from the films of slapstick genius Charlie Chaplin on a daily basis, both in regular speed and slow motion, in hopes that they would absorb the flavor of Chaplin's comedy.

In early drafts, therefore, *Snow White* was much more screwball than the final product became—the queen was fat, vain, and bumbling, and even Prince Charming was rather silly in his pursuit of Snow White. The dwarves changed personalities again and again, though proposed dwarves such as "Wheezy," "Deafey," and "Burpy" were thankfully discarded. Over time, however, Disney finally came to realize he should balance the comic scenes with emotional ones, making the queen more evil and frightening and the prince more sincere.

After almost two years of preparation—during which the studio continued to produce its *Silly Symphonies* in an increasingly desperate attempt to stay afloat—animation finally began. Disney ordered the comic material to be animated first, only then moving into the more emotional material; biographer Neal Gabler suggests that Disney in all likelihood wanted the staff to have as much experience as possible before tackling Snow White's apparent death.

Disney had always worked his staff hard, with an autocratic, occasionally arbitrary zeal. He had strict rules against romantic relationships between male and female staff, and disapproved of their drinking and parties to blow off steam. He lived and breathed animation, and expected his employees to share his obsession. Many of them did, in fact; everyone knew that Disney was changing the industry and producing something excitingly new, and this sense of accomplishment inspired his staff to push themselves still further.

But under the mounting pressure of this production, Walt Disney became more irascible than ever. He lashed out at any idea or sketch that he saw as less than perfect, but while Disney could always offer a specific, withering critique of someone's work, he rarely could tell them what to do instead; he was still groping for what he wanted, inventing an art form as he went. His staff therefore lived in terror, and at one point actually posted lookouts to warn of Disney's approach. Soon, they were nearing mutiny.

It is a Hollywood maxim that many of the best movies are made by people who absolutely hate each other, and this soon became the case on *Snow White*. In 1936, frustrated animators forced to make a film for Disney's birthday celebration on top of their other work produced a mock-pornographic short of Mickey Mouse having sex with Minnie. Disney smiled, applauded, and asked who had drawn it. When they foolishly identified themselves, he fired them on the spot and left the party. When one of *Snow White's* animators was caught in an affair with the dancer-model who was posing for some of Snow White's scenes, both the animator and dancer were almost fired, but saved their jobs with a hasty marriage. One of the lead animators is believed to have written a long, anonymous letter to a Hollywood newspaper (which printed it in full) mocking Disney's pretensions and eccentricity. Yet another disgruntled employee apparently left a note up in the office reading "STICK TO SHORTS." Despite an investigation that rivaled the Spanish Inquisition, Disney never learned who was responsible; many believed it was in fact his brother and business partner, Roy.

That would not have been surprising, for Disney Studios' prospects were looking bleaker by the day. United Artists had ended its distribution deal with the studio when Disney farsightedly refused to sign away television rights to his work in perpetuity, despite barely even knowing what television was. But with UA's financial support withdrawn, Disney Studios threatened to buckle under the exploding costs of *Snow White*. Walt had to mortgage his home to continue paying for the film, and by the time of *Snow White*'s premiere, Disney Studios was more than a million dollars in debt.

As the deadline for the film—Christmas 1937—approached, everyone involved began to despair, convinced it would not be finished on time. The existing animators were placed on punishing, round-the-clock schedules, and new trainees were hired to crank out the final, missing cels. When Disney despaired that Snow White was appearing as pale as her name, almost anemic, some of the women responsible for the inking provided a startling solution—they took out their makeup kits and applied rouge directly to the art on cel after cel. When Disney expressed amazement at the consistency of their dabs, one of the women is said to have replied coolly that they did it on their own faces every day; why shouldn't they be able to do it for Snow White?

Through tremendous exertions, the studio completed the film on time. At last, Disney faced the day of truth: the premiere that would either raise his studio to new heights or destroy it once and for all. On December 21, 1937, *Snow White and the Seven Dwarves* debuted at Carthay Circle Theatre in Hollywood. It didn't take more than a few minutes to realize they had a hit on their hands. The audience laughed uproariously at the jokes and applauded madly even for the credits and backgrounds. Walt Disney sat near the movie star Clark Gable, and saw him begin to cry at Snow White's apparent death. At that moment, he later recalled, he knew that the future of his studio was secure.

The film was universally hailed as a triumph by contemporary reviewers, and continues to be regarded today as one of the greatest movies of all time. Audiences returned to it again and again, setting a new box office record that was not broken until Clark Gable's turn in *Gone with the Wind*. Adjusted for inflation, *Snow White* remains one of the highest-grossing movies of all time even now. European crowds went similarly wild for it, and even the august Soviet auteur Sergei Eisenstein, the great pioneer of film montage, called it the greatest film ever made. Even if Walt Disney had never made another film, he would still be famous today simply for *Snow White and the Seven Dwarves*.

But even as Roy happily totaled the mounting profits from *Snow White*'s worldwide box office, Walt was back at his desk, sorting through ideas for a follow-up feature. Perhaps it was *Winnie the Pooh,* or *Alice in Wonderland,* or *Bambi*. It didn't really matter; he was only getting started.

Introduction

"All our dreams can come true, if we have the courage to pursue them."
—Walt Disney

Creative people have always been an object of fascination for society. Those who make things that are nearly universally beloved are not just honored, but studied with an equal degree of scrutiny as given to major players in history. Those who move mountains are often held in the same regard as those who paint them.

Not all artists, poets, and writers have pretty and idyllic histories, however. Edgar Allen Poe was a well-known alcoholic, Lord Byron was abused as a child and chronically depressed, and John Milton went blind for half of his life. While these kind of stories may make their triumphs seem greater when contrasted against their struggles, the fact that these were real people strikes a sympathetic chord in many.

Walt Disney had a decidedly awful childhood, often neglected and abused mentally and physically by an overbearing father. Driven by an imagination that forced him to create, he spent most of his life pursuing a childhood fantasy that had been denied to him.

Though he is known for the things he created, for the theme parks he built and the films he produced, Disney was not a simple man by any means. His strong convictions drove him to be recalcitrant, often surly, rude, and inconsiderate. He under paid and hardly ever credited or even complimented his extraordinarily talented staff.

Yet he also created an enormous range of childhood memories, moments that have endured for the better part of a century, films that shaped the way youths view the world and react to it, and played the hearts and minds of millions like a harp. His public image was traditional, and he was seen as an uncle to many people who felt as though they knew him through his productions and persona.

Despite this, he was a union-buster, possibly anti-Semitic, who indirectly disrupted the lives of many through his testimony in Washington, D.C. during the Red Scare. A participant in the age of McCarthy, Walt Disney was paranoid about communism, and firmly believed that those who espoused its virtues were responsible for many of his own hardships and failings.

The man himself exists in a strange dichotomy, equal parts jovial and draconian. The way the world views him varies based on popular opinion, which seems to shift each year.

What follows is an examination of Walt Disney's life, warts and all.

Chapter 1:
Early Life

> *"That's the trouble with the world. Too many people grow up."*
> —Walt Disney

From One Generation to the Next

Walt Disney was born December 5, 1901, in Hermosa, Illinois, a neighborhood on the northwest side of Chicago. He was the fourth son of Elias and Flora Disney. As is the case with most high-achieving individuals, his relationship with his father was complicated, and, at times, abusive. From his mother, Disney received a love for fairy tales, and the ability to use his imagination to escape the everyday reality of hard work and disapproval he was subjected to by Elias. His father was the son of Kepple Disney, a failed prospector, farmer, and free-spirit. Kepple Disney, Walt's paternal grandfather, had declined offer to become a partner in the sawmill owned by his own father, Arundel, on the shores of Lake Huron, in Canada.

Because of his hatred of the brutal Canadian weather, Kepple Disney moved his wife and children to southern California, in an effort to strike it rich in the gold mines. When he failed at prospecting, Kepple relocated his family to Ellis, Kansas, where he became a farmer. Of Kepple's two sons, Elias declined his father's offer to work alongside him and Elias's older brother, Robert, and decided, instead, to join a team of workers laying tracks for the railroad, which ran through Ellis.

When Elias found himself in Denver, Colorado he formed a band—he played the fiddle—and played on the streets at night for tips. He returned to Ellis after several months. His intention, however, was not to work on the farm with his father and brother. He wanted to get to know Flora Call, the daughter of the farmer who owned the plot of land adjacent to the Disney farm. Elias and Flora were married in the spring of 1888. He took a job managing a hotel in Daytona Beach, Florida. The Disney's first son, Herbert, was born that same year, followed by Raymond in 1890, Roy in 1893, Walter in 1901, and their last child and only daughter, Ruth Flora in 1903.

Shortly after Herbert was born, Elias left home to enlist to fight in the Spanish-American War. When he realized that he did not care for military life, Elias was able to secure a discharge due to a knee injury. Since he had also decided he did not care for family life either, he had to be coerced to return to Florida by an offer from his in-laws to buy him his own orange grove in the town of Kissimmee. He was content to remain a citrus farmer until the great frost of 1889 destroyed his harvest. Wishing to move farther away from Flora's parents, whom he found intrusive, he moved with his growing family to Chicago.

Elias found work as a handyman for a church, and soon became a member of the congregation. The pastor, Walter Parr, became a friend of Elias's, and he promised to name his next son after the minister, should he be blessed with another one, which is how Walt got his name. When their last child was born, Elias came to the conclusion that he was unable to abide the corruption, prostitution, growing number of saloons, and rising crime in the city of Chicago. He moved his family to Marceline, Kansas, a town one hundred miles northeast of Kansas City.

It has been reported that Elias was not actually opposed to the growing unsavory environment in Chicago, as the saloons (and the prostitutes who worked in them) were among his favorite pastime enjoyments. Some reports indicate that he was indebted to some of the unsavory characters who also frequented these places, and his inability to cover these debts influenced his relocation. Elias's brother, Robert, had purchased a fifty-acre farm in Marceline, and Elias joined his brother to work the land. His dissatisfaction with his life and his inability to make his fortune turned into what became a lifelong hatred of capitalism and what he imagined to be the exploitation of the working class of America by Jewish bankers. He instilled these beliefs into his children.

In 1906, Elias was able to buy an additional forty acres. He offered to his two oldest sons, Herbert and Ray, the chance to farm the land in return for a share of the profits from the season's crops when they were harvested. When Elias suffered losses on the harvest due to a surplus of apples, he was unable to pay his sons, who then decided to leave the farm, much to their father's dismay. Elias, who had always been a stern disciplinarian, given to fits of rage and physical abuse toward his sons, became even more so toward Roy and his younger brother Walt, who were sixteen and eight at the time.

Roy and Walt were expected to work the farm in their older brothers' absence, and were physically beaten by their father whenever he was displeased. On evenings when they weren't being punished, the boys' mother, Flora, read Walt fairy tales at bedtime until he went to sleep. Although he loved his mother, he was never able to understand why she didn't stop his father from beating them. His older brother Roy was the only person to comfort and reassure him.

When Walt was allowed rare instances of free time, he often drew pictures using a piece of coal and toilet paper, as paper and pencils were a luxury he was not allowed. Walt spent his time drawing the animals on the farm, as well as the landscape. In 1909, Elias suffered yet another set of losses, and became ill with typhoid fever. The fever developed into a case of pneumonia, and he had no choice but to sell the farm. He used the proceeds from the sale to purchase a thousand-customer newspaper route. Roy and Walt became delivery boys in their father's new business.

The business was marginally successful, requiring Elias to hire helpers, and Roy and Walt were rarely, if ever, paid for their services. When the newspaper business began to fail, Elias took out his frustrations on his sons.

On Roy's eighteenth birthday, he decided it was time for him to follow in his two older brothers' footsteps and leave home. Roy knew that Walt, who was only ten at the time and small for his age, would be left with no one to shield him from their father's rages. Before he left, Roy spent a great deal of time teaching his younger brother how to defend himself. The last time Elias raised a hand to Walt, the boy grabbed it and showed his father that he would no longer be abused. The beatings finally stopped.

Walt Disney Discovers His Love of Art and Theater

Disney was an average student, but he was an avid reader. He enjoyed his art classes, although his sketches were often unusual, and surprised his teachers. In 1912, Walt became friends with Walter Pfeiffer, a classmate with whom he performed in a school play. While spending time at Pfeiffer's house, Walt experienced fatherly kindness and acceptance when he grew close to his friend's kindhearted and loving father. Walter's father took the two boys to the movies often, and it was during those outings that he became a fan of Charlie Chaplin, whose work later influenced Disney's own work.

In 1917, Elias was able to sell the newspaper route. He used the funds to relocate his remaining family to Chicago, and to buy a share in the O-Zell Jelly factory. Flora pleaded with Elias to allow Walt to finish the school year in Kansas. She was able to persuade Herbert, her oldest son, to return from his travels to watch Walt for the remaining days of the term. Instead of returning to Chicago with his parents once the school year ended, Walt made the choice to wait in Kansas for the return of his brother, Roy, who had had his own travel adventures. Roy convinced Walt to apply for work as a news butcher.

As a news butcher, the sixteen-year-old sold newspapers, candy, cigarettes, and other items on trains during trips. He wasn't very good at his job, but didn't mind, since he was able to see much of the country, and to experience freedom he'd never had at home with his parents. When the summer ended, Walt returned to Chicago and enrolled for his junior year at McKinley High School. After submitting some of his drawings, he became the junior art editor of the school's newspaper. It was during this time that he enrolled in art courses at the Chicago Academy of Art. To pay for his classes, he worked part time at the post office, the Chicago El, and at his father's jelly factory.

That same year, Roy enlisted in the Navy to fight in World War I. He was twenty-four at the time. Walt went to visit his brother at the Great Lakes Naval Station outside Chicago, and returned home determined to enlist himself. Unfortunately, he was too young to sign up. Instead, he forged his parents' signatures and volunteered to go abroad with the International Red Cross. His mother, who had already seen two of her sons enlist, begged Walt to change his mind, but he was adamant, and left.

During his training in Chicago, Walt contracted the flu during the epidemic of 1918, and recovered just as the war came to an end. He was sent to France to drive an ambulance, and to help with the treatment of sick and injured soldiers. He was largely bored with his duties of driving officers and wounded soldiers in France, and spent his spare time drawing caricatures of his friends. He returned to Chicago with extra money in his pocket, and, although his father expected him to return to the jelly factory, eighteen year old Walt Disney had other plans.

Home Again to Kansas

Much to his father's disappointment, Walt returned to Kansas City, where he had spent much of his time as a young boy, and moved in with two of his older brothers. He got a job with a small ad company and began his career as a commercial artist with Pressman-Rubin Studios. He was assigned the task of drawing farm equipment. Unfortunately—and somewhat ironically—Walt was fired from the company a month later, due to his lack of drawing skills. It was due in part to this turn of events that Walt made the decision to continue his studies with a course at the Kansas City Art Institute.

As a matter of expanding his knowledge of drawing, theater arts, and films in general, Disney also began to borrow library books detailing anatomy, motion, animation, filmmaking, and character and story development. He practiced the technique of drawing each individual frame onto white linen paper and mounting each frame on pegs. The frames were then shot with a camera one at a time, creating the illusion of movement. Using a borrowed camera, Disney began making his own animated films in the evenings and on weekends, convinced he could make better short films than the ones he saw in theaters.

While Walt was employed at Pressman-Rubin, he met and befriended Ub (short for Ubbe) Iwerks. Iwerks became Disney's friend, collaborator, and business partner, a relationship that lasted for years. Ub had been fired from the ad studio shortly after Walt. The two collaborated briefly on a business venture, Iwerks-Disney Commercial Artists, but the business proved to be less than lucrative. When Ub saw an ad in the local newspaper advertising a job as a cartoonist at a company called Kansas City Ad, he recommended Walt abandon the business and apply. Walt was hired.

In time, Walt was earning enough money to live the type of life he'd only been able to dream of as a child. He was able to frequent movies as often as he liked, and spent a great deal of his free time in the movie houses that were popping up all over the city. When a job became available at the company, Disney recommended his friend Ub, who was hired, making the two coworkers once more.

At the age of 20, he was able to quit his job and form his own company, Laugh-O-Gram Films, Inc. He hired a salesman, a business manager, and four young animator apprentices. Just as Walt was beginning to do well and to build his business into a success, his parents came back to Kansas, and moved in with Walt and his brothers. Elias's jelly factory, as so many of his other ventures, had failed. Perhaps due to his own failures, he was convinced that Walt's business would collapse as well.

Disney and his father were complete opposites. While Elias was stern, cold, and had an aversion to people, Walt was fun-loving, charming, and gregarious, if somewhat shy. Walt, as an adult, was determined to make up for the childhood he had been denied, and vowed to never be like his father. The arrival of his parents reunited the entire family, except for Walt's older brother, Raymond, who was a traveling insurance salesman. The reunion was cut short, however, when Roy developed an acute case of tuberculosis, and was advised by his doctor to move to a warmer climate. He moved to New Mexico. Walt's oldest brother, Herbert, was transferred from his position with the Post Office to Oregon, and took their parents and younger sister with him, his wife, and children.

Since animated films at the time were typically shorts played before a feature film in theaters, they were soundless and produced with cut out animation. Walt Disney invented a process for creating new animated films that included live-action footage of real people inserted into the shot. Laugh-O-Gram received an order for six animated short films from a distributor in New York City, but when the work was delivered, the distributor failed to pay the company, and Walt was unable to pay his bills and his staff.

Sleeping in his office, bathing at the train station, eating canned beans and the occasional free handout from a nearby Greek deli, and working largely without help, Disney, who believed in his idea, produced a film called Alice in Cartoonland, an animated short film starring a local six-year-old child actor and model named Virginia Davis, whom he had met while employed at Kansas City Ad. The films consisted of the live-action scenes of Virginia as Alice, filmed against large drawings.

He wrote to a distributor in New York, hoping to secure a deal that would save his company. When a distributor expressed an interest in seeing the finished Alice films, Disney and Ub attempted to complete the work before their funds were depleted. Unfortunately, the two were unable to make payroll, pay rent, buy supplies, or hire extra help, and Laugh-O-Gram—true to Elias Disney's prediction—folded in 1923. Walt then decided it was time to move. He narrowed his choices between New York City, where the very best animation houses were located, and Los Angeles, where Roy had taken up residence, and was recuperating nicely. Walt chose California, and, with his last $40, booked a first class ticket to travel to the West Coast.

Chapter 2:

Success and Betrayal

"The way to get started is to quit talking and begin doing."
—Walt Disney

Westward Bound

In the summer of 1923, Walt arrived at the doorstep of his Uncle Robert's home in Los Angeles. While Walt's father Elias had remained in the Midwest, Robert had settled on the West Coast. Robert and Walt had never met, but he allowed his young nephew a room in his house at the rate of five dollars per week. Roy was living in the Sawtelle Veterans Hospital in west Los Angeles, still recuperating from tuberculosis. His first act as a California transplant was to visit his brother.

Walt, who had grown weary of animation, explained to Roy that he had decided to make an attempt at movie directing. After trying for weeks to secure a position at one of the major studios and being unable to find work, Robert, who had sold vacuum cleaners door-to-door upon his arrival in Los Angeles, advised his nephew to "get a real job." While Walt was considering taking his uncle's advice, he received a telegram from a New York City film distributor, Margaret Winkler, who had heard his pitch for the Alice movie, and who wanted to know how the film had turned out. Disney sent her the unfinished film, and she ordered twelve short films, at a price of $1500 each.

When Disney told Roy about the telegram from Winkler, he was skeptical. But since he loved and wanted to support his younger sibling, Roy offered to help with the venture. He gave Walt $285 as an investment. With an additional loan of $500, Walt was able to begin production on the ordered films. Roy eventually overcame his apprehension and grew to love Walt's enthusiasm. He and Walt set up The Disney Brothers Studio in the back of a real estate office, with Walt serving as the creative idea man, and Roy functioning as the business and financial manager. Roy left the hospital and the two brothers moved into an apartment together.

Margaret Winkler had some requirements for the films. She insisted Disney use the same girl who had appeared in the unfinished film, as well as requesting improvements on the camera work, which she felt was a bit "shaky," and the animation. The brothers enlisted the help of Roy's fiancé, Edna, who was still living in Kansas City, to appeal to little Virginia Davis's parents. The Disney brothers were offering them a contract of $100 per month to relocate to California and allow their daughter to star in the films. They agreed, and production began in earnest the day after the family arrived.

The first film, Alice's Day at the Sea, which was filmed at Venice beach and was more live-action than animation, proved to be satisfactory to Winkler. She sent the first $1500 installment, but advised Walt that the animation and camera work were still inferior. For the next film, Disney rented better equipment, hired temporary help to do the filming, and set out to convince his long-time friend and collaborator, Ub Iwerks, to move to Los Angeles.

After the failure of Laugh-O-Gram, Iwerks had returned to Kansas City Ad, and was receiving a salary of $50 per week. Walt initially offered him a salary of $20. Iwerks agreed to move to California only after Walt promised him $40 per week and shares in Disney's newly-formed company.

Although Iwerks completely reworked the animation portion of the Alice movies, and shifted more of the focus to the cartoon characters, the first two movies did not perform as well as the distributor had hoped. Unable to find jobs, Virginia Davis's parents demanded Disney raise her salary, and Margaret Winkler threatened to either lower their fee from $1500 per film or to cancel the contract altogether. With Walt obsessed with figuring out why his movies weren't doing as well as they'd hoped, Roy took over negotiations with Winkler.

Roy discovered that the Alice movies were, in fact performing very well. Margaret Winkler had recently married and turned over control of her film distribution company to her new husband, former Warner Bros. booking agent, Charles B. Mintz. Mintz's first act was to lower all payments to the company's film suppliers. Aware of the success of the films, Roy was able to negotiate an even better contract for the Disney brothers, and for the first time since the company was formed, they began to make a profit.

The staff had grown from a two-man operation to an enterprise employing over a dozen animators, filming crew, and salesmen. The company needed to move to a bigger office. After they relocated to a bigger space on Hyperion Avenue, not far from Hollywood Boulevard, Walt announced that the name of the company was being changed from The Disney Brothers Studios to Walt Disney Studio. While not happy with the change, Roy continued to support his brother.

The Disney Brothers Find Love and the Studio Finds a New Home

In April of 1925, Roy and Edna were married, with Walt acting as best man. The success of the company allowed the brothers to purchase homes, new automobiles, and to live, at last, in relative comfort. Since Edna had no friends yet in Los Angeles, Roy arranged for one of the company's female employees to serve as maid of honor. That employee, Lillian, was an ink-and-paint girl (one of the very few positions females were allowed to hold at the company at that time), making $15 per week.

Walt found Lillian lovely, and they began a relationship. The courtship between Walt and Lillian was brief, and just three months after Roy and Edna's wedding, Walt married the twenty-four year old. The wedding took place in Lillian's hometown of Lewiston, Idaho, and was attended only by the bride's mother, as Walt's parents were not physically able to make the trip, and Walt was at odds with Roy. The couple returned to Los Angeles, where they began their married life.

Shortly after the company moved into the new offices, Charles Mintz paid the Disney brothers a visit. He claimed that the Alice movies were selling so poorly that he could no longer continue his contract with them. He left, and Walt fell into a depression that lasted for two days. Unbeknownst to the Disneys, Mintz had made a deal with Carl Laemmle of Universal Pictures to produce a series of shorts starring an animated rabbit. Mintz concluded that the Disneys would be so desperate for continued work that not only would they create the character, they would need him to take the helm of their company. He was only correct on one count, however, and the Disney brothers set to work creating the character for Mintz.

With the Disneys unaware of the side-deal in place between Mintz and Laemmle, they created Oswald the Lucky Rabbit. Oswald bore a slight resemblance to the most popular animated character at the time, Felix the Cat.

While Walt took over the creation of Oswald's story, Ub perfected the drawings. The first cartoon produced by the studio was hated by Laemmle, whom the brothers still had no idea was orchestrating the deal behind the scenes, and Walt and Ub set to work recreating every aspect of Oswald's production. In the end, Laemmle ordered one film, although he thought the entire undertaking was a waste of time.

When the first Oswald film, Trolley Troubles, was released, it was a smashing success, and received rave reviews. Mintz created an entirely new company, whose purpose was to secure Oswald movies for Universal. Mintz then signed Disney to a separate contract with his new company, giving Mintz full control of Oswald. He ordered a new Oswald film from Disney every other week, and had the payment of $2250 per film hand-delivered by his brother-in-law, George Winkler. Winkler was allowed to freely roam the halls of the Disney building on his stops to deliver checks, and to pick up finished films, and so was privy to the growing dissatisfaction among the Disney employees. He reported his findings back to Mintz.

Although Universal had offered a contract for 26 Oswald episodes (presented by Mintz, of course), the employees at Wald Disney Studios were growing tired of the extended hours, extra work, and low pay offered by Disney. They were also dismayed at his seeming inability to share credit, or to recognize the contributions of the staff. While Roy attempted to stand in for Walt by offering his appreciation, the staff felt Walt should be more concerned about their grievances. Walt's inability to understand the feelings and needs of his employees came to be a shortcoming that plagued his company for many years.

When Walt learned of the deal between Mintz and Laemmle, he was extremely angry. He also learned that the two had merchandized Oswald, leaving the Disney brothers and their company out of that aspect of the deal entirely. When Walt told Roy of the arrangement, he advised him not to "rock the boat," and reminded him that their company was, in fact, performing the services they had contracted to perform, and that business was better than it had ever been. He explained to Walt that the merchandise actually benefitted their company, as it led to higher ticket sales. Walt was still not pleased.

Betrayal and Loss: Walt Says Goodbye to Oswald

In 1928, Walt and Lillian went to New York to meet with Mintz regarding the renewal of the Oswald contract. After a pleasant lunch that included their wives, the men returned to Mintz's office to discuss the renewal. Mintz informed Disney that he would be drastically reducing the per-picture advances, and that if Disney did not agree, Mintz would take control of all Oswald productions, and would hire most of Disney's staff to complete the work. Frustrated and betrayed, Disney was unable to continue the discussion, and simply left the meeting.

Roy informed Walt by phone that Mintz did indeed own Oswald the Rabbit, and also that four of the company's most talented animators had handed in their resignations to go and work for Mintz's company in New York. There was nothing the brothers could do about any of it. Mintz later offered Disney a contract with yet another Mintz company, in exchange for a 50% share of Disney's company. He gave Walt a month to decide. Desperate, Walt reached out to Mintz's wife, Margaret, the woman who had given him his start, to ask for her help. She advised Walt that she was no longer involved with the business, and that he should accept her husband's offer.

Unsure of what to do, Walt returned to his hotel room and attempted to sleep. In the early morning hours, he received a call from his brother. Advised by Roy to relinquish all Oswald rights to Mintz and come back to California and start again, Walt did just that. He and Lillian left New York City the next day. Disney returned to Los Angeles with no distributor, no Oswald, very few of his staff remaining, and very little money.

On the train ride home, Walt began to imagine a new character to replace Oswald. He knew that the future of Walt Disney Studio depended on coming up with something spectacular. While animation at that time was extremely basic, violent, and created by older men for crude audiences, Walt wanted to create a more family-oriented, fun-loving character, suitable for enjoyment by audiences of all ages.

Disney began sifting through ideas, and was inspired when the train he was riding made its way through the town of Marceline, Missouri, where the few happy childhood memories Walt had were formed. He'd lived in Marceline with his family for five years, from ages four through nine, and was revived by the site of the only place he'd experienced anything resembling a childhood. The visit helped him to regain his focus.

When he returned to California, although he was still affected by a sense of loss and failure, Disney rallied again, with the help of his brother, Iwerks, who had remained at the company (having been awarded stock, and having worked his way up to a $120 per week salary), and the remaining employees. He held daily brainstorming sessions, determined to create a character that would be even better than Oswald, and which his company would own, in whole. Disney vowed to never again work on a character of which he did not have complete ownership and control.

Chapter 3:
Making Mickey

"Mickey Mouse popped out of my mind onto a drawing pad 20 years ago on a train ride from Manhattan to Hollywood at a time when business fortunes of my brother Roy and myself were at lowest ebb and disaster seemed right around the corner."

—**Walt Disney**

The Creation of Mickey Mouse and "Talking" Cartoons

On his return to Los Angeles, Walt and Ub set to work creating a new character. Using "character sheets," the two listed all of their ideas.

The way in which they arrived at using a mouse for their character remains the subject of much disagreement and conflicting reports. According to one legend—the one most readily accepted—while on the train ride home from New York City, Walt remembered a pet mouse he kept in a cage at his desk at Laugh-O-Gram. Having made friends with the creature, one of many who reportedly gathered in the artist's trash can at night, Walt became fond of the rodent. Once the decision was made to use a mouse, Walt wanted to call him "Mortimer." Lillian, however, disliked the name, and suggested "Mickey."

Ub Iwerks' son, Dave, has asserted, however, that once Disney returned to California, the two created the iconic character together, with Mickey's look being the sole design of Iwerks, who was the better illustrator. Either way, it's agreed that Iwerks modified one of his Oswald drawings, shortening the ears and rounding the eyes, and the face of Mickey Mouse emerged. In 1928, the studio started working on the first Mickey Mouse cartoon. The work was done in complete secrecy—Walt had learned his lesson regarding protecting intellectual property. He had also developed an unfortunately deep sense of distrust in his employees.

Since the company still owed Mintz three final Oswald films, Walt left the work to the staff, and he and Iwerks handled the bulk of the production on the Mickey film. Iwerks, the only person Walt trusted besides Roy, was given greater responsibility for animation and character creation. Disney preferred to be free to develop stories and to keep a closer eye on the rest of the staff. Disney's friendship with Iwerks eventually ended due to Walt's inability to give the loyal Iwerks credit for his creations. Roy again advised Disney to acknowledge Ub's contributions, but was reminded by his brother that Roy's job was to look after the books, and that Iwerks was fine.

When the final payment for the Oswald movies was received and Disney's relationship with

Mintz was finally severed, the studio had enough funds to produce three Mickey Mouse short films. The first two, Plane Crazy, inspired by Charles Lindbergh's trans-Atlantic flight, and Gallopin' Gaucho, a loosely-reworked version of the first film, were not well-received by audiences. After two unsuccessful sneak preview screenings, Roy suggested the films needed more work, but Walt felt the films were good as they were. He attempted to secure a distributor, but was unable.

For his third and final attempt to launch his new character, Disney put the mouse on a steamboat, with a love interest. Inspired by the success of The Jazz Singer, the first "talkie" film, and frustrated by their inability to find distributors for their first two Mickey projects, Walt decided to use the new synchronized sound technology to produce the first animated talking short film. He hired an old acquaintance from Kansas City, Carl Stalling, to compose music for the production.

While in New York City searching for a suitable sound recording system, Walt met Patrick Powers, a former Universal executive, who had developed his own sound system, using the DeForest Phonofilm system he had failed to acquire as a prototype. Combining Stalling's score with Mickey's movements and voice (which Walt himself provided), with popular, well-known tunes such at Turkey in the Straw, Disney and Powers arranged a private screening for New York film distributors.

During the time Walt was in New York finishing the film, the studio itself was in financial crisis. Roy, ordered by Walt to "do whatever it takes," sold Walt's beloved Moon cabriolet sedan to pay the bills and make payroll. Because of the addition of sound to the picture, Steamboat Willie cost the studio nearly twice as much to produce as the first two films. Unfazed by the costs, Disney insisted that Mickey Mouse would solve the studio's financial problems once and for all, once the film was released, if only he were able to secure a distributor.

After exhausting most of his resources, Walt was able to secure a deal with a small, independent distributor. The distributor owned his own chain of theaters, and offered Walt $500 per week, with a two-week guarantee, if Walt would show the film exclusively at his theater. Although he was reluctant to show the film to the public with no distribution deal in place, fearing it would hurt his chances at selling the film should the audience dislike it, Walt agreed, knowing he was in urgent need of the $1000 payment. Steamboat Willie opened at the Colony Theater on November, 1928. It was the opening short for a film called Gang War. Audiences loved the film.

After receiving rave reviews from critics, the film made Walt Disney the first animator to produce and release a commercially successful "talking" cartoon. Mickey Mouse became a phenomenon, and Disney had secured his place in Hollywood. Unfortunately, in his newfound celebrity, Disney failed, as usual, to share the credit for the incredible achievement with the one man who was most responsible for helping him: Ub Iwerks. Ub's resentment grew deeper.

As the financial collapse that precipitated the Great Depression neared and an anti-Hollywood sentiment developed, studios and distributors, who were eager to change the public perception of Hollywood as corrupt, amoral, sinful, and morally bankrupt, courted Walt with offers to purchase the rights to the wholesome, family-friendly character. Walt, however, was still bitter from his experience with Mintz and Laemmle, and was determined to retain his independence and ownership of Mickey Mouse.

When Carl Laemmle called to request a meeting with Walt, Disney was unable to resist the temptation to find out what his old adversary wanted, and agreed. Laemmle offered Disney financing, national distribution and use of the animators that had left Walt Disney Studios during the Oswald debacle. Walt, with a great amount of personal satisfaction, turned down Laemmle's offer, because Laemmle wanted to own the copyright to Mickey Mouse.

While he felt a sense of gratification at being able to deny Laemmle, Disney was still without a distribution deal.

Walt Makes a Deal and Loses a Friend

When Pat Powers offered Disney a deal that would allow Pat the right to distribute the Mickey films on a "states' rights" basis. This kind of deal meant that the films would be distributed to individual, independently-owned theaters, instead of being distributed through the major studios, who controlled their own national chains of theaters. Powers agreed to pay Disney $2500 per film for each new movie, if Disney would agree to give Pat ten percent of the gross profits of each film, and Disney's promise that the studio would continue to use Powers' Cinephone sound system. Disney made the deal, much to the dismay of Roy, who, after reading the fine print of the contract realized the studio now owed Powers $26,000 per year for ten years of the use of the system. Walt stood by his decision.

Over the next eighteen months, the studio completed thirty-one talking Mickey films, which Mickey Mouse more famous than even Felix the Cat. In an effort to reach an international audience, Walt planned and produced a series of animated shorts called "Silly Symphonies" that featured music and very little dialogue, effectively removing language barriers. Neither Roy nor Powers cared for the idea, but as always, Walt pressed forward. When he finished the first film, The Skeleton Dance, Walt, along with his brother-in-law, William Cottrell, attended a screening to assess the audience's reaction. The film was an instant hit.

As time progressed, Roy continued to voice his concerns about the contract with Powers to his brother, who continued to ignore them. Although the "Silly Symphonies" films were commercially successful, the studio was experiencing cash flow problems, and the

Disney brothers themselves were earning far less from the films than they should have been. In spite of Walt's unwavering belief in Powers, Roy hired an independent accountant firm to monitor attendance at films, and to verify whether or not the studio was being cheated. While Roy tried to get to the bottom of the discrepancies, Walt, who was growing more nervous, stressed, and exhausted daily, was growing weary of creating the Mickey films.

Disney began to take out his frustrations on Ub Iwerks, his most trusted and loyal friend and employee. When Walt was scolded by his wife for being so harsh with Ub, he insisted that his friend was fine. During a meeting held to confront Powers about the fact that he owed the Disney brothers more than $150,000 in receipts from the Mickey Mouse films, Powers declared that Ub Iwerks had signed a contract to work for Powers. Walt was completely blindsided.

Powers used Iwerks as a bargaining chip, informing Walt and Roy that if they made him the head of their operations, he would give them back Ub, and give the two brothers a weekly salary of $1500 each. Realizing it would cost more to recover the owed monies through the court system, not to mention the amount of time it would take, the brothers declined the offer, and, although Powers owed them, the two settled with him for the amount of $50,000, just to be rid of him. With the terrible relationship with Powers behind them, Walt and Roy prepared to move forward.

Depression and Restoration

A few months after resolving the Powers conflict, Lillian Disney walked into her bedroom to find Walt had collapsed to the floor, unconscious. After being rushed to the hospital and having his stomach pumped, it was revealed that Walt, who had grown increasingly nervous and anxious, had been taking sleeping pills. Their family doctor expressed to Lillian deep concern that Walt was having a nervous breakdown. It was more likely that he was in a severe state of depression over recent events that included the loss of Ub Iwerks, escalating production costs, and overwork. Walt followed the advice of his doctor and took a sorely needed break.

Along with Lillian, her brother, and his wife, Walt traveled by train to New Orleans, Washington D.C., New York, and Key West, Florida, where the two couples boarded a ship and sailed to Cuba for a week. Their vacation continued in Panama, where they boarded a private yacht to sail back to California. By the time they returned to Los Angeles, Walt was back to his normal self.

In 1931, Walt Disney received two nominations from the Academy of Motion Picture Arts and

Sciences for Oscars in the specially created category of Best Short Subject for his "Silly Symphonies" short, Flowers and Trees, and the Mickey Mouse short, Mickey's Orphans. Both awards were given to Walt, who again neglected to thank Ub Iwerks, probably due to the fact that he felt completely betrayed by his old friend, who was still employed by Pat Powers.

Disney in Color

That same year, Disney became interested in making his first color cartoon, feeling that it was time for a new innovation to boost the studio's reputation and sales. He began to investigate a new technology called "Technicolor," a new three-color process that would allow studios to produce films in color without the prohibitive costs and brief shelf life of the "tinted" films of the past. Ub Iwerks, who was in the process of forming his own animation studio, had been to the Technicolor laboratory, and it was rumored that he would be releasing his own color animation short. Roy, who was against the added costs colorizing the films would incur, hoped Walt would forget the idea. Of course, Disney was undeterred.

Against Roy's objections, Walt made a deal with Technicolor, and ordered his Oscar-winning "Silly Symphonies" short, Flowers and Trees, be scrapped and remade using Technicolor. The change resulted in an increase in orders for the film as well as new ones. Unfortunately, the rise in orders did not make up for the rising costs of production due to the addition of color, and the studio found itself, once again, in financial crisis.

After a series of licensing deals with various businessmen, Disney realized he was not seeing the profits from Mickey Mouse novelty items that he should be, and formed an in-house marketing team at the studio. It was the business acumen of Herman "Jay" Kamen, whom Disney hired to run the new division, which resulted in major profits from the sale of Mickey and Minnie Mouse themed merchandise, and rescued the studio from what would have surely been economic collapse.

In order to keep the studio stocked with animators, Disney employed the services of former soldier, Don Graham, a talented artist working at Los Angeles' Chouinard's Art Institute, to teach classes at a building adjacent to the Hyperion Avenue Disney studio. Graduates often became apprentices for the studio, providing Walt with a stream of talented employees, at a free or highly discounted rate of pay. While the live action actors featured in Walt's films often became celebrities, the animators were largely kept anonymous, and rarely received individual recognition for their work.

While Walt had signed a deal with Columbia Pictures to purchase Disney cartoons for an advance of $7500 each, the rising costs of production made it necessary for him to approach the head of the studio, Harry Cohn, in an effort to raise the advance to $15,000. Cohn flatly refused. In the midst of the Great Depression, Cohn was experiencing money difficulties of his own. When Walt suggested they end their business relationship, Cohn ripped up their contract right on the spot. The termination of the contract left Disney responsible for paying back the $50,000 loan the studio had taken out from Columbia to pay Powers off. Payment was required in full, at that time.

When he heard of Walt's predicament, Carl Laemmle, his old nemesis, offered to pay the debt and distribute his films at whatever price Walt demanded. The only catch was that Walt would have to relinquish the copyright to

Mickey Mouse. Walt was dangerously close to accepting his offer when producer Joseph Schenk of United Artists offered Disney the $15,000 per picture he was seeking, plus a sliding percentage of the profits on all films. While Schenk's offer was generous, there was a very good reason for it.

Schenk was part of a collective that included Charlie Chaplin, Douglas Fairbanks, D.W. Griffith, and the actress Mary Pickford that joined together to create United Artists as an alternative to the big studio system. Although the company was proficient at movie distribution, the lack of real structure made making movies difficult for the group. Seeing the potential of adding the Disney's studio to their ranks, the group was eager to help Disney avoid the pitfalls of dealing with the notoriously crooked Laemmle, with whom Disney had already had a profoundly negative experience. The new deal allowed Disney to return to making movies, free from financial worries—for a while, at least.

Chapter 4:
The Full-Length
Feature

"Of all the things I've done, the most vital is coordinating those who work with me and aiming their efforts at a certain goal."

—**Walt Disney**

Walt Disney and the "Golden Age of Animation"

Feeling somewhat legitimized by his Oscar wins, Disney decided to shift his focus to more innovative animation techniques. Among his first actions was the creation of a story department for the studio. He then hired storyboard artists to guide future projects.

In the absence of Ub Iwerks, Disney decided to update Mickey's look, giving him a larger head, round stomach, and small limbs, making the character appear more like an infant. While adding color had given a new dimension and depth to his cartoons, he was intent on allowing his characters to show emotion. Mickey was drawn with more expressions, giving him a more realistic facial appearance. Whereas the old Mickey was somewhat aggressive, the newer, kinder Mickey was more childlike in his actions.

In 1933, Lillian announced that she was expecting a child, and Walt purchased a new house for their growing family. In celebration of the coming baby, he decided to make a film for his wife. Remembering that he'd been considering making the story of the Three Little Pigs into a movie for some time, Walt determined to make a ten-minute feature of the story, and wanted to portray an emotional depth not before seen in animation.

Walt and Ub Iwerks had attempted to make the story of the Three Little Pigs years before, but discovered that the story did not translate well in black and white. One of Disney's new animators, Norm Ferguson, presented Walt with a series of color sketches of the Big Bad Wolf, and Disney knew at once that the film would be a hit. Fred Moore, a self-taught artist and the youngest animator employed at the studio, was responsible for the drawing of the three little pigs. Disney had noticed his proficiency in drawing animals, especially pigs.

As production on the film continued, it was suggested that music be added to the film, and the studio's in-house producer, Frank Churchill, was enlisted to compose a soundtrack for it. After adding lyrics by fellow Disney employee Ted Sears, Churchill was advised that his work, depending on the reception of audiences, may be replaced by that of famous composers Ira Gershwin or Irving Berlin, but that he should go ahead and complete the work anyway.

When the film opened at New York's prestigious Radio City Music Hall in May of 1933, the reaction from the audience was lukewarm at best. Walt was disappointed and angry. However, when the film premiered in the smaller, more intimate settings of neighborhood theaters, audiences immediately fell in love with the film. The song "Who's Afraid of the Big Bad Wolf," written by Churchill, became a radio hit as well. It became a symbol during the Great Depression of hope and of the ability of the common people to triumph. That December, Lillian gave birth to their daughter, Diane Marie. At a private home screening of the film, Lillian informed Disney that she probably should have presented him with triplets. In 1936, the couple adopted a second daughter, Sharon.

With his successes mounting, Disney had finally managed to capture the interest of Hollywood's elite, who had been reserving judgment until they were certain Walt's luck wouldn't run out. Among his personal friends he counted the actor, Spencer Tracy, who taught him to play polo, and his boyhood idol, Charlie Chaplin. As he settled into his new celebrity status, Disney became dissatisfied with making short films. The profits from the Three Little Pigs merchandising allowed him to begin work on his most ambitious project to that point: a full-length animated feature film.

Snow White

One evening in 1934, Walt sent the staff of the studio out for dinner, advising them to return for a company meeting that evening. When the employees were assembled, anxiously waiting to find out the purpose of the meeting, Walt began a one-person performance of the story of Snow White and the Seven Dwarves. Playing every part himself, Walt illustrated the story he wanted the studio to bring to life in their first, full-length animated film. The staff was shocked, but excited to begin the huge, unprecedented undertaking.

Roy Disney was not at all happy about his ambitious brother's vision. He was convinced the movie would lead to the destruction of the studio. While they argued about the project, in the end, Walt—as usual—got his way. Disney became obsessed with the project. Roy was able to secure financing for the film from their long-time financial backer, Bank of America, but he informed Walt that the bank was extremely unsure of the venture, and would not tolerate any delays or extra expenses. Walt agreed to the terms, although he was more concerned about how to present the movie to audiences in a relatable way.

Disney understood that the way to make audiences connect with the film was to provide as much realism as possible. He provided advanced training, visual references, and provided live models to his animators in order to give them the necessary tools to make their drawings as life-like as possible. He hired a dancer to perform for the animators, so that they could study her actions and duplicate them on paper. The process of animating Snow White and the Seven Dwarves was innovative and daring. It slowed down production and drove costs up. Disney didn't care.

In order to complete the film, the staff of the studio swelled to nearly 600 people. The influx of employees required the brothers to secure more workspace, and to provide the staff—which often worked around the clock—with living quarters. Roy was tasked with figuring out how to placate the financers, make sure payroll was met, and to keep the production moving financially. With ten months to go until the film's premiere date in December of 1937, the film had yet to be filmed, as the artists were still working to perfect the drawings. The film took three years to complete, and nearly bankrupted the studio, but Walt never lost faith in the potential success of Snow White.

When the budget grew exponentially and production stretched into the third year, the press and public began to ridicule Disney. They called the film "Disney's folly." Roy was concerned that the film may be the one to finally put the studio out of business. With staffers putting in ten to twelve hour days for minimal wages and with little recognition, the atmosphere of the studio grew tense. The drawings were not completed until the end of November, and with the premiere set for December 21, many wondered if the film would be ready.

When the film was released in December of that year, the 2.3 million dollar spectacle was a raging success, and became the highest-grossing film of 1938.

The defining moment for Walt was when, during the premiere, audiences wept genuine tears at the supposed death of Snow White. Disney knew that his film had caused the audience to forget they were watching a cartoon and that the film had connected with their emotions every bit as much as a live action film would have. He felt both vindicated and relieved. His experiment had worked, and his instincts, as usual, had been spot on. Walt was awarded honorary degrees from both Harvard and Yale, as well as the University of Southern California.

Their newfound financial success allowed Walt and Roy to move their elderly parents to Los Angeles and to buy them a home. In the fall of 1938, Elias and Flora were poisoned by carbon dioxide when the heating system of the house malfunctioned. While Elias survived, Flora was unable to recover. Walt never spoke of his mother's death, and turned his attention, instead, to working.

Snow White and the Seven Dwarves was followed by the simultaneous creation of three films: Bambi, Pinocchio, and Fantasia. The studio wrestled with trying to make Pinocchio a likeable character—in the original story, he was not. Walt decided to make the story about the puppet's desire to become a real boy. Both Bambi and Pinocchio were groundbreaking films in terms of their ability to suspend audiences' belief that they were watching animation instead of live action. Pinocchio was also the first animated film to realistically portray underwater scenery. But while Walt was satisfied with the progress of the two films, he was more interested in the creation of a third project, Fantasia.

Fantasia began as a cartoon short starring Mickey Mouse that was based on a symphony called The Sorcerer's Apprentice, which featured an orchestra led by composer Leopold Stokowski. Disney was so impressed with the project that he determined the film should be feature-length. He and Stokowski selected 8 symphonies, and the Disney team of animators created the visuals that would accompany the music. After the realism of his last three films, Disney was delighted to take on a more abstract concept.

With all three films being produced at the same time, there was a need to add an additional 400 staff members to the studio, bringing the total number of employees over 1,000. Disney knew that additions to the Hyperion studio would not suffice. The company needed to move to a larger space. While Roy was away in Europe, Walt purchased a 51-acre plot of land in Burbank, and began to plan the studio of his dreams. The campus contained a theater, a restaurant, a soda shop, a gymnasium, a gas station, a barber shop, and a three-story animation building, which also contained Walt's office on the top floor. In December of 1939, the move from Hyperion to Burbank began. When Roy returned, the brothers once again fought bitterly over the expense. Walt, as usual, was undeterred.

Walt Disney Studios Goes Public

The production of Pinocchio, with Walt's insistence on using only the latest animation technology, as well as developing new techniques in-house, had production costs twice the size of the costs of Snow White. The film was adored, but failed to turn a profit. Once again, the studio was in financial trouble. The brothers had to borrow from Bank of

America to finance the construction of the new studio. Roy convinced his younger brother of the need to take the company public. In April of 1940, the company went public, offering shares and raising 4 million dollars in capital. The brothers were, for the first time, offered guaranteed salaries: Roy a salary of $1000 per week, and Walt a salary of $2000 per week.

Part of the necessity of the public offering was the commercial failures of the studio's last two films, Pinocchio and Fantasia. With World War II raging in Europe, the studio lost a large portion of its audience. Also, many films were unable to show Fantasia, due the fact that the soundtrack required the theater to have a specific sound system. Along with these problems, the staff at Disney Studios was beginning to resent the working conditions imposed upon them by Walt. Growing dissatisfaction with pay, hours, lack of recognition, and the unpredictable, sometimes despotic temperament Disney was known to display was threatening to boil over into a full-scale conflict between the employees and their boss. Disney once explained why he failed to credit his staff for their work: "We allow no geniuses around our studio."

Although the new campus was complete with perks and amenities, those privileges were reserved for the staff members at the highest levels of the company, who were all men. Management was strict in their observance of company policy, and the atmosphere of the studio ceased to be a peaceful, creative one, and changed into one of unhappiness and resentment. Disney remained deaf to his employees' complaints.

The public offering allowed employees, for the first time, to have knowledge of the salaries of their coworkers. They were dismayed to know that salaries ranged from twelve dollars per week, to Disney's own salary, which was almost one hundred times that of the women working in the ink and paint department. By 1940, Walt was no longer the affable, gregarious boss most of the older employees had known in the Hyperion days. The studio began to feel more corporate and less family-oriented.

Unionization Comes to Hollywood

In the late 1930's, behind-the-scenes workers in Hollywood began to organize and form unions to demand better wages and other benefits, and The Screen and Cartoonist Guild began to organize animators and those working at animation studios in order to fight for fair wages. By 1940, Disney's studio was the last one remaining with no union, although it employed most of the workers in animation.

Disney was unbothered by the threat of unionization.

Arthur Babbitt, an animator who had been with Disney for nearly a decade and one of the studio's highest-paid animators, sympathized with the plight of his fellow workers, many of whom were barely able to live on the meager wages Disney was paying them. When the Screen Cartoonist Guild attempted to organize in the studio, Disney decided to demand his workers refuse to take part in the organization. Walt gathered the staff and made a speech, during which he minimized the staff's complaints, and basically made a case for the favoritism and classism he frequently showed. His speech seemed to blame the employees themselves for their lack of upward mobility. Disney's speech had the opposite of his intended effect, and the Screen Cartoonist Guild had no problem recruiting members.

When Arthur Babbitt joined the union, he represented the highest-ranking employee at the studio to openly support unionization. Walt was incensed at what he considered Babbitt's betrayal. Disney terminated Babbitt's employment that spring due to his union activities. The following evening, members of the staff who belonged the union voted to take action, and began a worker's strike on May 29, 1941. The strike effectively ended the "Golden Age" of animation for Disney.

With the strike intensifying daily and nearly half of his art department not working, stock in Walt Disney's company had dropped significantly, and due to the fact that both Pinocchio and Fantasia had failed to earn, the studio was in financial trouble once more. Bambi had not yet been released, and the strike was further delaying its progress. Disney refused to negotiate or to apologize to the workers. In fact, he did not acknowledge the strike in any way. After a physical altercation with Babbitt, Disney took out an ad in the trade newspaper, Variety, and accused Babbitt of being a communist. Disney left Hollywood for a ten-week trip to South America, essentially dumping the strike in Roy's lap.

While Walt was in South America, his father died. Disney declined to end his trip to attend his father's funeral. Roy was more than happy to have his younger brother out of the country so that he could handle the strike situation with no interference. Roy agreed to almost all of the strikers' demands, and was able to get the art department back on schedule by the time Walt returned to the country.

When World War II erupted, much of the studio's lot was commandeered by the United States Armed Forces. The studio managed to stay in business due to government contracts to make propaganda and training films. However, there was no funding for feature films, due to the war efforts, and Disney Studios was at a creative stand-still. After nearly five years, Disney felt the time was right to complete and release Bambi, one of the films the studio had been working on when the strike took place. When it was released in 1942, the movie failed to make back the investment. Disney blamed the war.

Realizing that the war, unionization, and changes in world consciousness had altered the view of his animated films, Walt began to rethink his over-investment in animated features. His company in shambles, deeply in debt, and hated by critics, and the artist community, disillusioned, depressed, and paranoid, Walt Disney realized it was time to take a new approach.

Chapter 5:
War, Politics, and Depression

"I'd say it's been my biggest problem all my life...it's money. It takes a lot of money to make these dreams come true."

—**Walt Disney**

The War Affects the World of Disney and Animated Films

After the strike and the start of the war, things at Disney Studios began to change. The time of experimentation and innovation gave way to a different style of moviemaking. Walt began to focus on a style of storytelling that leaned more toward the American folktale rather than classic fairytales. Walt chose The Tales of Uncle Remus, by Joel Chandler Harris, as his next project, which he titled The Song of the South. For this film, Disney reverted to the cost-effective art of mixing live action with animation that had given him his start. One reason for this change was the loss of financial backing for his full-length animated features. Bankers were no longer willing to risk money on the studio's ventures.

With the stories set on a plantation in the South following the Civil War, Disney was forced to display those issues in the film, which many found tone-deaf and insensitive, especially considering the facts that Jim Crow laws were still very much in effect at the time, many African-Americans were still being denied basic rights as American citizens, and Southern white supremacist groups were determined to enforce segregation. Disney sought advice from many famous and political African American leaders of the time, including the head of the N.A.A.C.P., who told him that he would do well to avoid the stereotype of the cheerful former slave, whistling and singing tunes and telling stories in spite of the pervasive racism.

Seven years after the premiere of Gone with the Wind, another Civil War-era film that had done very well, Disney premiered Song of the South at the same Atlanta, Georgia theater. While the actors who played the white roles in the film were all present, the actor who played Uncle Remus, James Baskett, was not allowed, by Georgia law, to enter the theater. Opinions of the film were polarized. Major news outlets like the New York Times panned the film, and the N.A.A.C.P. called for boycotts of the film. As usual, Disney was shocked by the criticism. He insisted the disapproval of the film was agitated by communists, whom Disney believed had been trying to destroy him since the strike.

In 1947, a rival animation studio, United Productions of America, became popular, and threatened to further change the landscape of animation that Disney had so carefully constructed, and of which he was the reigning king for so many years. UPA fought against the realism Disney pushed so hard to have his animators attain. UPA's animators were influenced by the modern art of the day, and dared to imagine abstract concepts in animated entertainment. The major problem with UPA, as Walt saw it, was that the staff consisted of his arch nemesis, Arthur Babbitt, and a number of animators who had left Disney after the strike.

Walt Disney Goes to Washington

After the war, when Hollywood was again subjected to union activities, Walt was determined to stop the progress of the unions before they could have an adverse effect on his studio for a second time. He was one of the founding members of the Motion Picture Alliance for the Preservation of American Ideals. The group was formed to protect the movie industry from what Disney called "communists, radicals, and crackpots." Walt was invited to Washington D.C. in 1947 to testify before the House Un-American Activities Committee, the body notorious for tracking and attempting to wipe out communists, or "Reds."

The Committee wanted to investigate the cause of the recent rash of strikes in Hollywood, and called Walt, along with several other high-profile entertainment personalities as a "friendly" witness. Walt was certain that there were no communists working at Disney Studios at the time, but took the opportunity to name Herbert Sorrell, a one-time animator at the studio, as one of the people he believed was a communist, due to Sorrell's involvement in organizing the 1941 strike seven years earlier. Disney, along with other entertainment personalities such as Gary Cooper, paved the way for Hollywood's major studio bosses to stamp out the unions once and for all by creating an environment for the so-called "Red Scare" to infiltrate the movie business.

The Cold War and Fear-mongering

Following World War II, fear of the rise of communism led to the second incarnation of the "Red Scare," which had first taken place between 1919 and 1920, when fear that the socialization of workers and political radicalism would lead to attacks and anarchy among the American people. In 1920, after the September 2 bombing of Wall Street during which 38 died and 141 were injured by suspected communists and anarchists, a series of criminal syndicalism laws were enacted to allow officials to arrest, detain, or deport immigrants who were suspected of "Un-American" activities. The laws made no distinction between communism, socialism, anarchism, or social democracy, and seemed to quell the violence and unrest taking place in the country.

The 1947 re-emergence of the Red Scare was prompted by the fear of communist activities being carried out in America due to tensions between the U.S. and the Soviet Union. That same year, the House Un-American Activities Committee, made anxious by the rise in striking and union activity in Hollywood, determined to find and stamp out any communist uprisings they feared may take place. The committee's aim was to identify and list all suspected communists.

While a group of actors, actresses, and directors denounced the hearings as illegal and unconstitutional, the committee pressed forward, aided by the testimonies of Disney and others who shared his point of view that the unions were out to undermine the American way of life. The witnesses who refused to participate with the committee's agenda were named the "Hollywood Ten," were found in contempt of Congress for refusing to testify, and were jailed as a result. These events led to the later forming of a "Black List," an unofficial list of performers, writers, actors, directors, and others that banned them from employment in Hollywood, due to their suspected communist ties. Although Disney was not directly responsible for the Black List, he contributed to the hysteria that allowed its creation.

Walt Leaves Politics and Finds a Hobby

After his testimony, Disney left the public eye briefly, and decided that he had no place in politics. He was anxious to return to making movies. By 1948, Disney was producing live-action films, including Treasure Island and So

Dear to My Heart, a story of rural America at the turn of the century. It was at this time that Disney began to wonder if there was any room for his productions in a new medium: television. He went to Alaska to film a nature documentary, Seal Island. By narrating the footage and creating a story, he was able to make the documentary more like one of his animated films. Seal Island went on to win an Academy Award, and opened the door for Disney to produce a series of nature documentaries called True Life Adventures.

After a successful run on television, Disney wanted to return to making feature-length animated movies. Roy, weary of placating his brother, adamantly refused, saying the features were too expensive to produce, with no guarantee of a profit. He and Walt had their most combative battle up to that time, ending with Walt telling Roy to either find financing for the films or he would force him to sell the company. Roy left, but later acquiesced, as he always did, to Walt's wishes. He found a way to raise the necessary 2 million dollars for their next feature: Cinderella.

After bullying Roy into allowing him to make the film, Walt seemed to lose interest in the production, and allowed his staff to be responsible for the majority of the work. He was beginning to feel the physical effects from not only aging, but from over two decades in the entertainment business. He hired a private nurse to work for the studio, and to give him back and hip treatments daily, due to an old polo injury. Hazel George, his nurse, became a friend and confidante to Walt.

While Disney had achieved far more than he'd ever imagined possible, he was unsure of the future of his company, and of his ability to ever create a phenomenon to rival the success of Snow White. His insecurities, together with his growing list of physical ailments, caused him to lose interest in the studio he had so lovingly and painstakingly created. That fall, ordered by his doctors to take a vacation, Walt left in the middle of production on Cinderella to attend a railroad convention in Illinois. He invited one of his animators, Roy Kimball, along for the trip.

Growing up, the railroad ran near his family's home in Kansas, instilling in Walt a love of trains. Shortly before his trip, he had installed an enormous toy train system in his office at the Disney studio. The train ride to Chicago along with his anticipation of the convention lifted his spirits immensely. When Disney returned to Los Angeles, he commissioned the building of a large scale model train at the Burbank studio. He spent much of his spare time in the studio's machine shop, supervising the construction progress. The head machinist gave Walt his own bench and tool set, and allowed him to work on the train himself.

In spite of being largely ignored by Disney, Cinderella's premiere in 1950 garnered rave reviews from critics and audiences, who had missed the classic Disney style of animation. The film grossed nearly 8 million dollars for the studio, which made Roy Disney exceedingly happy. Walt was happy to be financially solvent once more, although he was unimpressed with the quality of the film. Two other features were released by Disney studios after Cinderella: Alice in Wonderland and Peter Pan. While Peter Pan eventually earned a modest profit, Alice was yet another costly failure. Fortunately, the returns from Cinderella allowed the studio to withstand the economic ups and downs.

Nevertheless, Walt was too busy building another scale model of a train at his home, complete with a replica of his family's Marceline barn, to be overly concerned with the film. He built the tracks, engine, and engineered the setup by himself.

In 1952, Walt Disney began to liquidate some of his assets. While Lillian wasn't sure what he was up to, she knew he was caught up, once more, in a whirlwind of imagination. He sold the family's vacation home, borrowed against his insurance, and licensed the use of the name "Walt Disney Productions." He formed an entirely separate business, and began making plans for what became the greatest venture of his life.

Chapter 6:
Disneyland

> *"Why would I want to be president of the United States? I'm the king of Disneyland."*
>
> —**Walt Disney**

Disney Conquers Television and Creates a Fantasy Land

In January, 1953, Walt Disney formed a new company, Walt Disney, Inc., and made himself, his daughters, and his brother-in-law the principal owners. Lillian refused to be a party to her husband's shenanigans, and, as an act of revenge against Roy for his lack of faith in his latest idea, Disney excluded him. He later changed the name of the company to WED Enterprises.

Walt had created his WED company to come up with ideas. He had drawn up plans for his latest idea, one he'd been pondering for years. He'd been looking for a place where he could take his children for enjoyment, but the carnivals and circuses of the day were filthy, staffed with dirty men and menacing people, and the grounds were always disgusting. Walt wanted a place where families could go and be safe and have fun in a clean, wholesome environment.

Disney was constantly adding ideas to the plans for what he originally called "Mickey Mouse Village." He decided "Disneyland" was a better name. The plans grew larger and more grandiose every day. Disney wanted to use a lot he owned next to his studio, but as the plans grew, he realized the lot wouldn't be big enough. He began assigning different studio staff members to WED to work on the project. Of course, Roy wasn't on board when he found out about Walt's idea.

Typically, the carnivals that were popular at that time featured fast rides, unsavory characters, and a generally lawless atmosphere. Disney wanted to create a fantasy world that allowed people to belong to it, just as he had placed his live-action actors in the make-believe worlds he animated. The construction of the park would follow the same process as his construction of the miniature railroad he had built on the studio lot. Walt wanted to bring the scenery from his animated movies into reality. The problem he was facing was how to acquire funding for the project. To come up with the money, he hatched another revolutionary idea.

Since television had become popular, Disney had been trying to find a way to take advantage of that popularity. In 1950, he produced and hosted a one-hour Christmas special called "One Hour in Wonderland" in an attempt to promote one of his films. The program was so successful that television's three major networks clamored for Walt to provide them with more television programs since that time.

However, it wasn't until Walt realized the potential of television to provide a source of capital for his Disneyland project that he began to take their offers seriously.

Roy went to New York in 1953 to pitch ideas to the networks in order to secure a deal. He presented the idea of the studio producing a weekly show for one of the networks in exchange for the network proving the 5 million dollars needed for Walt to bring his latest creation to life. Although plans for the park existed, Roy felt he needed a detailed drawing to be able to sell the idea. Roy informed Walt of the need, and he begged one of his former artists to help him move the idea of the theme park from his mind onto paper. For the next two days, the pair worked together around the clock to come up with the drawing.

Even after receiving the drawing, Roy found it difficult to sell Walt's idea. NBC and CBS passed immediately, leaving only ABC. Although ABC was desperately in need of television programming that would move the network out of its third place ranking, it still took Roy months to convince the network to finance the park. With the reputation of the studio, much of his own personal fortune, and the very existence of his company on the line, Walt forged ahead, just as he'd always done. He believed in Disneyland, just as he'd believed in Mickey Mouse, Snow White, and the many other cutting-edge imaginings that had made him one of the most successful animators of all time.

The site for the park had outgrown the mere 5 acres originally owned by Disney, and had expanded to a 168-acre building site, which had been moved to Anaheim. Plans for the park included one million square feet of asphalt walkways, 5,000 cubic yards of concrete, and acres or flowers and shrubbery, along with a smaller-scale replica of an old-fashioned Main Street—one that reminded Walt of Main Street in his boyhood hometown of Marceline, man-made rivers, and an eighty foot Bavarian-style castle that towered over everything. More than a mile of railroad track would circle the park, and there would be a twenty-foot wall separating Disneyland from the rest of the world.

In the early 1950's, many families, having left the inner-cities and moved to the suburbs, were experiencing greater prosperity. They had more discretionary income, more leisure time, and were able to afford more activities. The generation of children born immediately following the end of World War II, the Baby Boomers, were, at this time, school-age. Families were looking for a fantasy place to which they could escape, a vacation destination that was suitable for all ages, where both children and adults could enjoy themselves. Disneyland was born at the perfect time.

Disney used television to create anticipation for the coming theme park. By creating programming that showcased Disneyland as a magical land of fantasy and dreams, Walt was able to make the audience feel as though they were a part of the creation of something special. Walt became a television personality that was loved by both children and adults for his ability to relate to them with a sense of sincerity and honesty. He always spoke to children as though they were his equals, and to adults as though they were his personal friends while he was on camera. He became everyone's "favorite uncle."

The hour-long Disneyland television show highlighted a different area of the park each week, and also told a new story on every episode. Adventureland, Tomorrowland,

Fantasyland, and Frontierland were the basis of the stories offered by the show, tying in the program with the four areas of the park. Excitement for the park was at all-time high. It was the episode on Frontierland that contained a story that struck a chord with every child watching. The story of wild frontiersman Davy Crockett became an instant hit.

Davey Crockett Explodes

Aired on three occasions from December of 1954, through February of 1955, Davy Crockett became the outspoken, truthful, and adventurous hero the public wanted. He embodied the ideals of the American values that Walt Disney espoused. While Crockett was anti-authoritarian, his propensity to follow his sense of right and wrong and to always do the honorable thing was a lesson parents were more than happy to have taught to their children. Ratings grew and grew for the series.

The show's theme song, "The Ballad of Davy Crockett," became a radio hit. There was even merchandising, as children across the country began wearing coon-skin caps.

Spending the majority of his time at the Anaheim site, Walt walked the park daily, giving orders and making changes, additions, and fine-tuning the details of what he termed his "living movie." He wanted to make sure the story made sense, and that the visitors to the park would be completely immersed in the experience. He was hands-on with his participation, even pitching in to paint scenery or build props.

As usual, Walt's project was over-budget, and his constant need for perfection pushed his staff to exhaustion. Six weeks before the park was supposed to open, the park's staff began to panic at the fact that the park may not be ready in time. The landscaping, paving of Main

Street, and the castle that brought the whole thing together were still unfinished. Nearly half of the planned attractions were still unable to function, the animated features of the park were not yet installed, and the staff asked Walt to push back the opening. He refused.

The construction crew of 2,500 men was working nearly around the clock, and the original 5 million dollar projected cost of the park rose to 17 million. Walt was unbothered. He was as excited before the opening of the park as he had been at the premieres of each of his many animated hit films. ABC planned to broadcast the opening of the park, the largest live-telecast ever attempted at that time, involving 29 cameras, dozens of crews, and miles of cable. The night before the opening, Walt could be found spray-painting back drops and walking the grounds.

Disneyland Opens to the Public

The park opened on its scheduled date of July 17, 1955. An extremely hot and uncomfortable day, the opening was not without its troubles. With traffic to enter the park backed up for seven miles, and the temperature nearing 100 degrees, counterfeit tickets being circulated, and the ABC filming crews experiencing technical difficulties, Walt was as elated as he'd ever been. His daughter, Diane, noted that she'd never seen him so happy. Although Fantasyland was closed due to a gas leak, Mr. Toad's Wild Ride was without power, and the female patrons in high heels were sinking into the still-soft pavement, Disney considered the opening a success.

Disneyland was opened to the public the day after the live broadcast. In its first ten weeks, the park was visited by 10 million men, women, and children. That number eventually settled to five million per year. The park became an attraction for foreign dignitaries who visited the U.S., and political leaders from all over the world stopped in to see Disney's wonder. Normal, everyday families were drawn to the park seeking a sense of escapism, a break from the everyday struggle. The "small-town America" feel of the park, along with its traditional atmosphere was in line with the values of middle-America at the time.

The themes contained within the park itself were consciously engineered by Walt, each with a specific purpose. Frontierland and Adventureland celebrated America's past. Fantasyland urged park patrons to explore their own imaginations, and to allow themselves to be lost in the magic of the park itself. Tomorrowland explored the future's technological and scientific advances.

Disneyland was a complete escape from the present. Disney kept an apartment on the grounds of the park, and spent much of his time there, as opposed to his actual home. He was able to walk around the park without being recognized by the patrons, and would often stand in line with them, hoping to get clues as to how he could improve their experience.

Disney visited the town of Marceline, Missouri in July, 1956. The town had served as the inspiration for many of Disneyland's idyllic features. The town planned to honor both Walt by naming a park in his honor, and he and Roy surprised the ceremony's planners when they accepted the invitation. Both of the Disney brothers were given a "hero's welcome" on their return, and Walt was thrilled to be so loved by the little town in which he held such wonderful memories, although his time there was brief. This visit was, in a sense, coming full circle for Walt's entire life.

Disneyland produced a steady income for Walt Disney, allowing him—for the first time in nearly four decades—to be free from worries about money and pressure from bankers and investors. The studio was producing television shows and specials, and continued to produce six feature-length films per year. Disney was aware of the fact that he, along with the body of work he'd created over his many years in Hollywood, represented a specific ideal. The Disney name represented a certain reputation for wholesome, family entertainment, American values, and quality work. He knew he was a symbol.

While he understood the fact that his name had become synonymous with family entertainment, he also felt restricted by the symbolism his company had come to evoke. After viewing the film To Kill a Mockingbird, Disney realized he was restricted in the content he could put out into the world. His misgivings, however, did not deter from the fact that he was extremely proud of all he'd accomplished.

When ABC considered dropping his television show due to low ratings, Disney moved the show to NBC, and began to build on the persona that encompassed all that the Disney name meant to the American public. He was, however, aware of the differences between the private Walt Disney and the personality he showed the world. He once said, "I am not 'Walt Disney.' I do a lot of things 'Walt Disney' would never do. 'Walt Disney' doesn't smoke—I smoke. 'Walt Disney doesn't drink—I drink."

While Walt tried to remain as "normal and ordinary" as he saw himself, he could not deny the fact that he could not be the same person in the public that he was in his private life. Walt was known for announcing his presence in the studio with a loud cough, thereby allowing the staff to put things in order before his "walk-through" would begin. While he was aware of his personal power and its effect on the people around him, in the end, he enjoyed his celebrity.

Walt Disney and the Billionaire

In 1953, following the success of Seal Island, Disney made his first full-length True-life Adventure film, The Living Desert. The film, a documentary that chronicled the lives of desert wildlife, was produced by the same team that produced Seal Island, was to be distributed by RKO Pictures, the studio owned by eccentric billionaire, Howard Hughes. Hughes, who was very much against nature films, and considered the natural habits of wildlife too unhygienic for public consumption, refused to distribute it, although he had distributed several short nature films prior.

Hughes, who had lost a great deal of money on Disney's films following Cinderella, had lost faith in Disney's features, and was reluctant to back The Living Desert for that reason, as well. Walt accused Hughes of being in breach of their contract, and went to visit the increasingly reclusive mogul. When Walt arrived, not only did Hughes release Disney from his contract with RKO, he attempted to sell Disney RKO outright, with a 10 million dollar line of credit.

While Walt wanted to make the deal immediately, he decided it would be best to talk to Roy first, which turned out to be one of Walt's most beneficial decisions. Roy conducted an investigation into RKO's finances. Not only had the studio become unprofitable due to Hughes's non-involvement and negligence, even with the 10 million dollar credit line, acquiring the studio would have plunged the Disney's into debt, with little hope of getting back to profitability. Walt turned the offer down in person, and Disney Studio's relationship with RKO ended.

Walt was done dealing with distributors; the RKO debacle was the last straw. Soon after the end of the RKO deal, he announced the formation of Disney Studios' own distribution wing, Buena Vista, and released The Living Desert on his own. The film, although less visually spectacular than Disney claimed, became the studio's second hit of the 1950's, and went on to receive the 1953 Oscar for "Best Documentary Feature." Even more exciting than the Oscar to Walt was the fact that he no longer had to share profits with an outside distribution company.

The Mickey Mouse Club

In 1955, with the success of the Disneyland television series secured, Walt Disney had an idea for a series that went on to become a part of television history: The Mickey Mouse Club. The show was a variety show that catered to children, developed by Disney producer, Bill Walsh. The show aired on ABC for an hour each week, beginning in 1955, and running, intermittently through various incarnations, until 1996, when it last aired on what became (and remains),the Disney Channel, a cable television staple.

The show format remained the same: a cartoon featuring Mickey, music, a newsreel, a story, and musical and comedy numbers. The cast was an ever-changing mix of teenage performers called "Mouseketeers," who became known to audiences by their names via the "Mouseketeer Roll Call" at the beginning of each show. The actors would announce their first names during the show's opening. A signature of the show was the "Mickey Mouse Ears," a cap that was made to resemble the famous ears of Mickey. Many of the

Mouseketeers went on to have successful careers in Hollywood as entertainers.

Disney Studio Produces More Magic

Although Disney was busy with his theme park projects, the studio continued to produce films and television programs. Between 1955 and 1963, Disney studios produced more successful animated films including Sleeping Beauty, 101 Dalmatians, Lady and the Tramp, and The Sword in the Stone.

When the organizers of the American National Exhibit at the Moscow Fair of 1959 needed a presenter who displayed exemplary showmanship, they contacted Walt Disney. He created the most popular exhibit of the show, a nineteen-minute film called America the Beautiful that was shown in the exhibit's 360 degree theater. One year later, he was commissioned to plan and conduct the opening and closing ceremonies of the 1960 Winter Olympic Games in California.

Mary Poppins

By the time the 1960's began, the Disney studio was free of financial woes, running smoothly, and operating at its full capacity, but Walt was anxious to create something new. By the age of 61, Walt had won more Academy Awards than any other film producer in history, but with all he'd accomplished, he had never even been nominated for a "Best Picture" Oscar, a fact he intended to change. He had become obsessed with one particular story that was in development at the studio.

Mary Poppins was based on a children's book that was a favorite of Walt's two daughters when they were young. He had begun planning for the film twenty years earlier, and had left the project unfinished, as other projects took precedence. He had decided to revive the project, and to move forward with the film. He also decided to return to the live action/animation combination that had launched his career.

Disney wanted the film to focus on the story, and for the animation to drive the story forward. When Mary Poppins premiered in 1964, it became yet another of Walt Disney's instant hits. The film was nominated for thirteen Academy Awards, including a nomination for "Best Picture," the first for Walt Disney. With the nomination, Disney felt that he had, at last, been accepted and validated as a true filmmaker by the Academy.

The 60's and the Changing Times

By the time Mary Poppins debuted, the world was an entirely different place from when Snow White and even Cinderella were released. Between the "British Invasion," the discovery of folk music by the children who once visited Disneyland with delight (but who were now teenagers), and the escalating tensions caused by the growing Vietnam War, the wholesome, family-values driven public that had fueled the success of Disney's efforts up to that point were eroding. Much as it had during World War II, the country's consciousness evolved, and the attention of the public was shifted to more important concerns. Jim Crow, segregation and the Civil Rights Movement, now televised for the viewing public's consumption, further drew attention away from Disney's world of "make-believe." Life became very real for many of Disney's former fans.

Disney's films were either applauded for providing an escape from the current state of affairs, or criticized for being unrealistic, out of touch, and just plain corny. Disney's conservative values were no longer celebrated. Those values, which were often tinged with racism, classism and sexism, were the foundation on which the Disney Studios had built its public persona. Walt continued to ignore the growing gap between the very traditional 1940's and 50's and the more radical, liberal progression of the 1960's. He was out of touch, and didn't see the need to find a common ground. He continued his work in the way he saw fit.

Chapter 7:

Death and Legacy

"All the adversity I've had in my life, all my troubles and obstacles, have strengthened me... You may not realize it when it happens, but a kick in the teeth may be the best thing in the world for you."

—Walt Disney

Disney Plans Another Theme Park

In 1965, Walt Disney began buying land in Central Florida; as much as 27,000 acres had been purchased by the time he revealed his plans. Walt described the new project as "new and different from Disneyland," and called the project "Project Future." In reality, he was planning the "Experimental Prototype Community of Tomorrow," or EPCOT. He wanted to create something to leave a legacy that would last for the generations to come after him; he wanted to create a city of the future.

EPCOT was designed to be an example of what the cities of the future could achieve through the proper use of planning. Part of the plan was to completely enclose the entire 50 acre community in order to provide climate control. Disney planned to include the EPCOT center as part of the Disney World theme park, which would also include a "Magic Kingdom," an exaggerated version of Disneyland, hotels and resorts, shops, and golf courses.

The Formation of Cal-Arts

One thing Walt Disney prized was the training and education of future animators and artists. Having only been able to attend courses sporadically in the beginning of his career, Walt was largely self-taught, and wrestled with his lack of drawing ability on occasion. He made sure to staff the Disney studio with the best talent he could find, and had made an arrangement, in 1929, with Nelbert Chouinard, founder of the Chouinard Art Institute in Los Angeles, to provide instructors to Disney Studios for the purpose of training new animators. In 1955, Chouinard named Walt Disney to the school's board of directors.

Disney granted two two-year, full scholarships to deserving students through the Walt Disney Foundation. In the following years, the school came to depend on the Walt Disney Foundation for most of its funding, which it acquired through scholarships, and the arrangement with the studio to provide classes and instructors.

By 1960, the school was almost completely under Disney's control. By 1963, the growing number of academic classes—as opposed to the number of actual art classes—caused ongoing campus protests. Disney decided to merge the school with the California Institute of the Arts. The two schools combined formed Cal-Arts, which was patterned after the famed California Institute of Technology.

Disney pledged all of the profits from Mary Poppins to the creation of the new institute, and also donated thirty-eight acres of land the studio owned in Golden Oaks Ranch, a site just north of Los Angeles, to build a new campus. The groundbreaking ceremony for the new campus did not take place until 1969, with classes beginning in November of 1971. The campus contains The Walt Disney Theater, an indoor performance auditorium that was later renamed the Walt Disney Modular Theater.

Disney stated once, in an address to the school's students, "If you keep busy, your work might lead you into paths you might not expect...That happens in science; some of our most important discoveries have come from scientists who were searching for something else. What young artists need is a school where they can learn a variety of skills, a place where there is cross-pollination... The remarkable thing that's taking place in almost every field of endeavor is an accelerating rate of dynamic growth and change. The arts, which have historically symbolized the advance of human progress, must match this growth if they are going to maintain their value in and influence on society."

Cal-Arts offers courses and degree programs in film, video animation, puppetry, writing, theater, dance, music, and, of course, art. The school's philosophy is to provide a place where students are able to closely interact with their teachers, and combine disciplines for a more well-rounded education. The school is divided into three entities: the campus education and artistic program, the REDCAT (named after Roy and Edna Disney), the production, presenting, and exhibiting venue founded by the school in 2003, and Cal-Art's Community

Arts Partnership, which connects the school with other arts organizations to form partnerships that allow students to train to teach art.

Long after Walt Disney's death, his daughter Sharon continued to serve on the board of the school, and the Walt Disney Foundation continues to financially support the institution. Cal-Arts has awarded many honorary degrees since its inception. Past recipients include Beverly Sills, Roy Lichtenstein, Twyla Tharp, Harry Belefonte, Ray Bradbury, Annette Benning, Peter Sellers, Don Cheadle, and Disney's own nephew, Roy E. Disney.

In the summer of 1966, Walt took a vacation with Lillian, his daughters, Diane and Sharon, and his grandchildren. It was rare for Walt to allow himself to leave the studio, but he had been offered the use of a private yacht, and wanted to spend time with his family before he was plunged into the depths of the EPCOT planning and construction. The Disney family toured the western coastline of Canada, up to Alaska. It was during this trip that his family became aware of Walt's failing health. Noticing that he was coughing through the night, his daughter, Diane, became extremely worried about her father.

The World Grieves for Walt Disney

In October, 1966, Walt filmed a promotional film for EPCOT. During the filming, he was so ill, he was unable to breathe without the help of oxygen, which was administered between takes. The staff at Disney's studio began to notice he wasn't looking well, and that he was even surlier than usual. Along with pain in his neck and shoulder, the remnants of a long-ago polo injury, Walt was experiencing pain in his hip. He confided in his nurse, Hazel George, that he was in constant pain.

Disney, much to the relief of George, scheduled spinal surgery. Unfortunately, during the pre-surgery exam, it was discovered that one of Walt's lungs had a growth on it. Walt, who had smoked all of his adult life, knew what that meant. He was diagnosed with cancer, and given two years to live. Despite the prognosis, Disney felt that he could beat the disease. During his last visit to the studio, Walt viewed a rough cut of a film in progress, and advised his staff to "keep up the good work," as he exited the room. It was, by all accounts, the first and last time he ever praised his staff. He never returned to the studio.

Walt checked himself into the hospital, where he was visited daily by his older brother, Roy. On December 14, Walt told Lillian to leave the hospital in order to rest, assuring her that he was feeling better. Roy stayed behind, and Walt attempted to communicate to him his vision for EPCOT. The following day, December 15, 1966, Walter Elias "Walt" Disney died from complications due to lung cancer.

Disney's death was front-page news around the world. California's Governor, Edmund G. Brown stated, "I shall miss Walt Disney. Our state, our nation, and the world have lost a beloved and a great artist." Lillian received from condolences from President Lyndon B. Johnson, Ronald Reagan, and J. Edgar Hoover, director of the FBI. From great studio heads, to entertainers, to domestic and international news outlets, the world mourned the passing of "everyone's favorite uncle."

Although the rumor has circulated since his death, Walt Disney's body was not frozen. He was, in fact, cremated, and his ashes are interred at the famed Forrest Lawn Cemetery in the Hollywood Hills. Walt left half of his estate, which was then valued at $35 million, to his wife, Lillian. He also made her the executor of his will. He left the other half of his estate in trusts to Lillian, Diane, and Sharon. The rest of his assets were left to the Walt Disney Foundation, Cal-Arts, and his nieces, the daughters of his brothers, and his sister, Ruth. He left nothing to Raymond and Roy, his surviving brothers. He didn't like Raymond, and felt he had already made Roy a very rich man during his lifetime.

Disney Studios Enters a Turbulent Era

Walt's death created a leadership crisis for the studio that he had spent the better part of his life building. The studio was largely divided into two sides: the "creatives", who were loyal to Walt, and the "administrators," who were loyal to Roy. Roy voluntarily retired, and was replaced by two committees, each representing one side. Directors for each side were placed in charge, and the studio continued to flourish for several years under the agreed-upon system.

By the early 1980's, thanks to the overturning of the dual-leadership process, a change spearheaded by Roy's son, Roy E. Disney, the studio had been through a succession of leaders, and suffered financial losses due to the box office failures of films like Tron, and The Devil in Max Devlin. Along with the division at the studio came the reality that Walt's beloved EPCOT project had not opened along with the Disney World amusement park. Due to financial, legal and technical issues unforeseen by Walt, the opening of the "City of Tomorrow" had been delayed by eleven years. The cost had risen to an astounding $1.2 billion. Roy Jr. refused to attend the opening ceremonies, enraged that Disney's board of directors had approved the expenditure.

The studio suffered continued losses due to the leadership of Ron Miller, Walt's son-in-law by Diane, and Thomas Wilhite, a friend of Miller's who had been appointed to a leadership position after Ron's promotion to President and CEO of Walt Disney Productions following Roy Jr.'s departure. Roy E. decided to consult an attorney in an attempt to prevent what he was convinced was the destruction of the Disney legacy by Miller. He and attorney Frank Wells convinced Disney's board of directors to fire Miller, and replace him with Michael Eisner.

Eisner, who had been the head of Paramount Pictures at one time, had a proven track record of production success. He had increased Paramount's revenue from $100 million in 1973 to over $1 billion in 1984. Before he could take over as head of Disney, Saul Steinberg, a corporate raider who had been watching Disney's stock decline during the upheaval, attempted to acquire the company and sell off its assets, including the film library, the Burbank studio, and both theme parks at an enormous profit. In 1984, the company paid Steinberg $325 million for the stock he had purchased in the company. Although he did not make the profit he stood to make by dismantling the Disney Empire, he walked away with a profit of $31 million dollars in exchange for leaving the company intact and walking away.

The unrest coupled with the drastic reduction in the price of Disney stock forced Walt's widow, Lillian, to pay a visit to the company's board of directors to find out what was going on at her husband's company. After her visit, the board voted to remove Ron Miller from his position and re-instate Roy E., who had left the company, to the board. Miller, who was replaced by Stanley Gold, retired, and he and Diane moved to northern California, purchased a vineyard, and bought a sheep farm in Colorado.

Sharon, Disney's younger daughter, was never involved in the business at the studio. Sharon was involved in charity work, and was a member of the board of Cal-Arts until her death from breast cancer in 1993. Lillian Disney passed away from complications due to stroke in 1997. Diane died in 2013, after a fall from which she never recovered. Roy Disney, Walt's brother and business partner for most of their lives, died in 1971 after a seizure. Roy Jr. died in 2009, after a battle with stomach cancer.

In 1984, Michael Eisner, Frank Wells, and a young Jeffery Katzenberg were appointed to lead the studio, and completely revamped all operations. Under Ron Miller, the staff had grown uninspired and complacent. Many of the existing staff were either terminated or retired. By the next year, nearly 400 former Disney studio employees had been replaced by Eisner's hand-picked team, most of whom came from Paramount. Eisner also negotiated the purchase of the rights to the MGM/United Artist library, giving Disney the right to merchandise MGM products, and to use the MGM "Leo the Lion" logo. He also added several MGM-themed rides to the theme parks.

True to Walt Disney's revolutionary vision of combining live-action and animation, the studio, under Eisner, released a project that had been virtually ignored by Ron Miller: Who Framed Roger Rabbit. The film was the most expensive ever produced by the studio, at $52 million, with an additional $32 million needed for distribution and promotion. The film eventually grossed $328 million world-wide, and together, with Good Morning Vietnam

(1987), and Three Men and a Baby (1988), the studio, for the first time in its history, grossed over $1 billion.

Instead of being grateful for the new direction and prosperity of the studio, long-time Disney employees were bitter and disgruntled. They claimed the studio was attempting to push them out by converting to an almost totally computerized system of animation. Michael Eisner, for reasons that still baffle many, traded in his stock options for a reported $192 million in 1992, and left the company. In the years since, Disney has weathered storms as it always has, and triumphed over all.

The Man's Legacy

Walt Disney was a complicated man. Was he a racist? An anti-Semite? A hard-driving, work-driven, mad genius with a heart of gold? The opinions of the man himself fall on extreme sides of the spectrum. He is the man who declared, after his oldest daughter's birth, that orphans world-wide be allowed to see his films for free. But he's also the man who tried mightily to squelch the unions who attempted to organize his under-paid, over-worked, and under-appreciated staff.

Disney was the man who created fantasy lands still loved and adored millions. But he's also the same man that testified before the House Un-American Activities Committee, helping to set the stage for an era of paranoia, unfair and illegal proceedings, and the destruction of many careers and lives.

Walt Disney was a creative whirlwind, but he was also the man who never shared credit, and, often, took credit where perhaps it was not deserved.

However history records its memories of Walt Disney, the one thing that will remain constant in the relation of his story is that he was an idea man, a thinker who was brave enough to bring his visions to life, regardless of the cost. He was fearless. He was a perfectionist. By sheer willpower, he created a legacy of artistic revolution, and secured animation as one of the most lucrative and limitless mediums of modern-day technology. Walt Disney, whatever the means used to achieve it, is well deserving of his status as a cultural and creative icon.

Recognition

Walt Disney's achievements include more than seven hundred citations, honorary degrees, awards, and presentations. He received twenty-nine Oscars, four Emmys, the Irving Thalberg Award, the Presidential Medal of Freedom (the highest civilian award in the United States), and the French Legion of Honor. His animated films continue to delight children and adults of all ages, and the international chain of amusements parks that perhaps represent his greatest leaps of faith and imagination continue to provide a place of escape for park patrons from all corners of the world.

Believing strongly in his vision of presenting delightful, story-driven works in a visually appealing animated form inspired him to implement new art styles, technology, and color palettes that were previously unheard of. It was deeper than that however; he successfully married compellingly in-depth character development with top-tier storytelling and film scoring. It is an often said that things are always thought to be impossible until they are done. Walt Disney made the impossible possible.

Early in his career, Walt realized just how game-changing the use of sound, combined with lively, highly competent animation, and well-developed stories could be. Rather than chasing the trend of simply synchronizing music to animation, he pioneered the process of cultivating a soundtrack so deep, rich and complex, that the results threatened to top the efforts of live action films of that time. While very few studios were interested in the concept that he proposed, Walt was not deterred.

Through his partnership with Pat Powers and his Cinephone, Disney was able to implement the use of soundtracks that allowed actors to perform their scenes in front of a recording phonograph. The animation's speed was adapted to the speed of the audio recording, setting a precedent for audio synchronizing that remains in use today.

Walt was also savvy in regards to the need for innovation in animation techniques and the need to expand to a more realistic color palette. When he was first introduced to the concept of a three-color combination method offered by a fledgling company named Technicolor, he knew he needed to take advantage of the as-yet unused technology in a way that others did not dare. Because the company was not yet capable of servicing large-scale, live action productions at that time, he was able to negotiate an exclusive deal for his animated shorts. Disney's instincts proved to be correct, and he won an Academy Award presented for Flowers and Trees, an installment of his Silly Symphonies series.

Leading in the field of animation by a comfortable degree, Walt Disney was not satisfied to rest on his laurels. He was driven to create. His continued desire to test boundaries and to discover new territory drove him to pioneer a stereophonic sound reproduction system for what became the first commercialized effort to present a full-length, animated feature film in full stereo. The groundbreaking new system allowed music to be recorded in a way that focused on isolating audible elements, panning instruments to various parts of the auditorium and providing a more balanced sound.

Philanthropy

Today, Walt Disney is remembered for his love of people, although it was often thought that he preferred plants and animals. He has been quoted as having said that he wanted, above all, for his products be "people-centric." To date, Disney Companies have donated over $300 million to non-profit organizations, over 23 million books to schools, families, and children worldwide, and maintains various initiatives for schools aimed at increasing educational values.

Disney's philanthropic efforts extend to wildlife as well, with grant programs dedicated to the conservation of endangered and protected animals. The organization has given in excess of $25 million alongside the good will of many guests who contribute while staying at the related outdoor parks. Disney has also partnered with esteemed social groups like the Nature Conservancy that has allowed the planting of millions of trees. Not only concerned with wildlife, Disney is interested in the growth and maturation of genetic data research to further protect marine life as well.

Disney's charitable efforts can be traced back to Walt's understanding of the need to strengthen the reach of education and learning through leisurely play over sixty years ago. He worked with the Boys Club of America (which eventually grew and changed to the Boys and Girls Club of America), and the organization that become commonly known as the "Toys for Tots" program, offered through the United States Marine Corps. He also gave monetary help to the children's hospital St. Joseph's.

Disney charities have expanded their operations to programs that include working side by side with some of the world's most important and recognizable charities such as the Make-A-Wish Foundation, First Book, and the Starlight Starbright Children's Foundation. These partnerships have long since recognized that for many of their constituents, Disney products, including trips to Disney's theme parks, constitute the number one request. Disney is also known for volunteerism, and employees and executives have given a combined 667,000 hours to charitable efforts. Disney also offers a matching gift program for employees that ranges from $25 to $15,000.

Preserving Walt Disney's legacy of love for nature and all things outdoors, the company also strives to help the planet as a whole by innovating ways to decrease greenhouse emissions. This commitment is well-displayed at Disney World, where, due to the sheer magnitude of the parks' size, energy conservation is a primary concern, and first priority.

According to the 2014 Citizenship Performance Summary, the company has made great strides in decreasing park emissions by a reported thirty-one percent from just two years before, with no signs of slowing down. The goal is to bring that up to fifty percent by the year 2020. Aside from energy conservation, Disney seeks to reduce the amount of waste going to landfills by at least sixty percent. This goal, which many might consider out of reach, is already on track to be reached due to new technologies and processes that include turning waste into animal nutrition products, bio-gas, and fertilizers. Disney companies are more than cash-generating, heartless corporate entities.

Along with his contribution to animation, another facet of Walt's legacy extends to copyright law. Disney continues to lobby for extensions to its copyrights in order to maintain sole ownership of Mickey Mouse, a cause for which Walt fought tirelessly. Ownership of his creations became of paramount importance to Walt following his experience with losing one of his very first successful characters, Oswald the Rabbit. The laws Disney fought for continue to impact the creative industry to this day.

Disney's Contribution to Current Pop Culture

The influence that Walt Disney envisioned went far beyond merely creating memorable characters: he wanted to design a landscape and a world that was open to anyone. Through his films, television programs, theme parks, and his dedication to preserving the child in everyone, Disney provided the family-friendly escape from reality that has transcended boundaries and generational gaps to extend to the youth of current times.

The modern Disney has branched out to include its own cable channels, which have spawned several notable celebrities from any number of widely popular Disney properties, as well as its own radio stations, recording studios, and the Disney Music Group, which functions as the production arm of Walt Disney

Studios. A short list of celebrities that began their entertainment careers under the Disney umbrella includes:

- **Britney Spears**—Britney was a Mickey Mouse Club star who became a chart-topping pop star with several platinum records.

- **Lindsay Lohan**—Lindsay starred in The Parent Trap before making her mark in several high profile Hollywood movies.

- **Miley Cyrus**—Known primarily for her time as Hannah Montana, Miley has made her mark in music, following in the steps of her father, Billy Ray.

- **Shia LaBeouf**—The former Even Stevens star has gone on to helm such blockbusters such as Transformers.

- **Zac Efron**—Zac became a teen hearthrob during his time starring in High School Musical and hit Hollywood by storm with such top-tiered successes as 17 Again.

Disney's effect on culture is one that continues to evolve. As the world moves into a more digital age, the company has grown with it. The forward thinking that Walt Disney possessed was passed from one generation of Disney staffers to the next, and the Disney name is synonymous with quality, family-oriented content. The digital space allows for integration of Disney products into devices such as mobile phones, tablets, the internet at large, and in turn, reach young audiences they might not have otherwise.

Disney's expansiveness is no longer just in the titular name, but also in its reach. From Marvel to Pixar, LucasFilms to ESPN, Disney understands how consumers use mass media, and by capitalizing on this knowledge, the company continues to spearhead new technological advances including podcasts, online games, and more.

The companies started by Walt Disney nearly a century ago are the culmination of several factors: love, determination, a willingness to believe, and the understanding that, even though life can be distracting and sometimes discouraging, there is a place you can go to remember your fondest childhood memories and leave everything else behind. Walt would be proud.

Epilogue

"There's really no secret about our approach. We keep moving forward—opening up new doors and doing new things — because we're curious. And curiosity keeps leading us down new paths. We're always exploring and experimenting."
—**Walt Disney**

Walt Disney, animator, showman, and innovator, left a legacy unparalleled in many respects. From animation to pop culture, his imprint on the world will never be forgotten and continues to be celebrated by the young and the young at heart. Though his beginnings were humble, $40 and a dream were all that was necessary for him to create many of the most well-known and well-loved characters (such as Snow White and her attendant Seven Dwarfs, Mickey Mouse, and Winnie the Pooh) of all time. History will remember Walt for his many magnificent works to be sure, but arguably more than that, his memory will forever be treasured for his influence on the world at large.

The reality of Walt Disney was different from his public persona. He was disliked by his employees, but beloved by his family and those who watched his works or visited his parks. His views on society and politics make up a small but significant portion of his life story, and his contribution to the Red Scare will permanently be viewed by some as his defining moment.

But he was more than the things people have said about him; simply put, he's too big. The man was rich and poor several times throughout his life, and often survived due to nothing but sheer tenacity. His impact on society can never be understated. Countless children grew up watching films that he built from the ground up. Pinocchio taught them the dangers of lying; Bambi taught them to respect danger; Cinderella taught them that humble beginnings can lead to great things, and; Mary Poppins taught them how a father should act with his family. Countless other small but important lessons were portrayed through the works he created and those that were developed by his company after he left.

A man of his cultural influence can never be accurately summarized in simple terms of good or bad. The truth is that Walt Disney was a little of both. But whether he was naughty or nice, his positive impact on children across the world and the adults who rediscovered their own childlike wonder thanks to his works cannot be denied. Walt, in short, would be happy with his place in history.

Sources

Eliot, Marc (1993). Walt Disney Hollywood's
Dark Prince. New York, NY: Carol Publishing
Group

Mosely, Leonard (1985). Disney's World.
Briarcliff Manor, NY: Stein and Day,
Incorporated

Biography.com Editors. "Walt Disney
Biography" Biography.com Website June 24,
2016
Retrieved from
http://www.biography.com/people/walt-
disney-9275533

JustDisney.com "Walt Disney A Short
Biography" JustDisney.com
Retrieved from
http://www.justdisney.com/walt_disney/biogr
aphy/w_bio_short.html

Scully, Candy. "Walt Disney Part 1: American Experience." Published 21 May 2016

Scully, Candy. "Walt Disney Part 2: American Experience." Published 21 May 2016

The Walt Disney Company. "Philanthropy" TheWaltDisneyCompany.com 2016 ©Disney Retrieved from https://thewaltdisneycompany.com/philanthropy/

Goldhaber, Mark "Giving Back" mouseplanet.com 19 July 2006 Retrieved from https://www.mouseplanet.com/7151/Giving_Back

Williams, Tate "Disney Philanthropy: It's All About Animals" InsidePhilanthropy.com 25 November 2014

Retrieved from
http://www.insidephilanthropy.com/home/20
14/11/25/disney-philanthropy-its-all-about-
animals-and-nature.html

Cheeseman, Gina-Marie "Disney Vanquishes
Greenhouse Gas Emissions" TriplePundit.com
23 March 2015
Retrieved from
http://www.triplepundit.com/2015/03/disney-
reduces-greenhouse-gas-emissions/#

Sanford-Brown Blogs "How Walt Disney
Animation Revolutionized the Animation
Industry" SanfordBrown.edu 2 December
2014
Retrieved from
http://www.sanfordbrown.edu/Student-
Life/blog/December-2014/How-Walt-Disney-
Animation-Revolutionized-the-Animation-
Industry

Kurtti, Jeff "Wonderful World Walt: Walt And Animation Innovation" OhMyDisney.com 12 February 2013
Retrieved from
https://ohmy.disney.com/insider/2013/02/12/wonderful-world-of-walt-walt-and-animation-innovation/

Korkis, Jim "Award-Winning Walt" WaltDisney.org 12 February 2012
Retrieved from
http://www.waltdisney.org/blog/award-winning-walt

Imdb.com "Walt Disney Awards" imdb.com 24 June 2016
Retrieved from
http://www.imdb.com/name/nm0000370/awards